Gratitude Journal For Women

Julia Broderick

Copyright 2015 Julia Broderick - All Rights Reserved

How To Use This Book

Fill out a page from your gratitude journal every evening, before going to sleep. You will write about events that happened throughout your day. There is no perfect answer, just listen to yourself and write what you truly feel and what feels right for you. Filling out a page every day, will train your subconscious to focus on the beauty of the world we live in. Every 30 days, there will be a progression sheet in order for you to keep track of your growth.

In life, we are given choices, we can choose to focus on what we don't have, or focus on what we do have in our lives. We can live a life of dissatisfaction, or we can train our minds to focus on what to be grateful for. When we are grateful for the things we already have, the universe rewards us with so much more. When we learn to focus on what our obstacles can teach us, instead of the inconveniences they cause us, we achieve an outstanding level of freedom and finally live life the way we are supposed to!

For a free PDF version of my Self Confidence Journal For Women, type the link below into your internet browser

http://eepurl.com/bXkMuv

Our website:
www.beautifulhealthymom.com

For more books:
http://www.beautifulhealthymom.com/our-products/

Julia Broderick Social Media:

Youtube:
https://www.youtube.com/user/beautifulhealthymom1

Facebook:
https://www.facebook.com/BeautifulHealthyMom/

Twitter:

https://twitter.com/Beautyhealthmom

Date:_____

What I am grateful for:

_____
_____
_____
_____

What I have learned from my challenges:

_____
_____
_____
_____

Three things (big or small) that went well today:

_____
_____
_____
_____

Three beautiful things that I have noticed throughout my day:

_____
_____
_____
_____

~A moment of gratitude will change your attitude~

Date:_____

What I am grateful for:

_____
_____
_____
_____

What I have learned from my challenges:

_____
_____
_____
_____

Three things (big or small) that went well today:

_____
_____
_____
_____

Three beautiful things that I have noticed throughout my day:

_____
_____
_____
_____

~Live in the moment~

Date:_____

What I am grateful for:

_____
_____
_____
_____

What I have learned from my challenges:

_____
_____
_____
_____

Three things (big or small) that went well today:

_____
_____
_____
_____

Three beautiful things that I have noticed throughout my day:

_____
_____
_____
_____

~You have control of your life~

Date:_____

What I am grateful for:

_____
_____
_____
_____

What I have learned from my challenges:

_____
_____
_____
_____

Three things (big or small) that went well today:

_____
_____
_____
_____

Three beautiful things that I have noticed throughout my day:

_____
_____
_____
_____

~Learn to dance in the rain~

Date:_____

What I am grateful for:

_____
_____
_____
_____

What I have learned from my challenges:

_____
_____
_____
_____

Three things (big or small) that went well today:

_____
_____
_____
_____

Three beautiful things that I have noticed throughout my day:

_____
_____
_____
_____

~Be present, live in the now~

Date:_____

What I am grateful for:

_____
_____
_____
_____

What I have learned from my challenges:

_____
_____
_____
_____

Three things (big or small) that went well today:

_____
_____
_____
_____

Three beautiful things that I have noticed throughout my day:

_____
_____
_____
_____

~The root of happiness is gratitude~

Date:_____

What I am grateful for:

_____
_____
_____
_____

What I have learned from my challenges:

_____
_____
_____
_____

Three things (big or small) that went well today:

_____
_____
_____
_____

Three beautiful things that I have noticed throughout my day:

_____
_____
_____
_____

~In every misfortune, there's something to be thankful for~

Date:_____

What I am grateful for:

_____
_____
_____
_____

What I have learned from my challenges:

_____
_____
_____
_____

Three things (big or small) that went well today:

_____
_____
_____
_____

Three beautiful things that I have noticed throughout my day:

_____
_____
_____
_____

~Enjoy the little things in life, for the little things make the biggest impact~

Date:_____

What I am grateful for:
_____
_____
_____
_____

What I have learned from my challenges:
_____
_____
_____
_____

Three things (big or small) that went well today:
_____
_____
_____
_____

Three beautiful things that I have noticed throughout my day:
_____
_____
_____
_____

~Positive thinking creates positive outcomes~

Date:_____

What I am grateful for:

_____
_____
_____
_____

What I have learned from my challenges:

_____
_____
_____
_____

Three things (big or small) that went well today:

_____
_____
_____
_____

Three beautiful things that I have noticed throughout my day:

_____
_____
_____
_____

~You are greater than your obstacles~

Date:_____

What I am grateful for:

_____
_____
_____
_____

What I have learned from my challenges:

_____
_____
_____
_____

Three things (big or small) that went well today:

_____
_____
_____
_____

Three beautiful things that I have noticed throughout my day:

_____
_____
_____
_____

~Everything and anything is possible~

Date:_____

What I am grateful for:

_____
_____
_____
_____

What I have learned from my challenges:

_____
_____
_____
_____

Three things (big or small) that went well today:

_____
_____
_____
_____

Three beautiful things that I have noticed throughout my day:

_____
_____
_____
_____

~Life is beautiful~

Date:_____

What I am grateful for:
_____
_____
_____
_____

What I have learned from my challenges:
_____
_____
_____
_____

Three things (big or small) that went well today:
_____
_____
_____
_____

Three beautiful things that I have noticed throughout my day:
_____
_____
_____
_____

~Everyday is a chance for greatness~

Date:_____

What I am grateful for:

_____
_____
_____
_____

What I have learned from my challenges:

_____
_____
_____
_____

Three things (big or small) that went well today:

_____
_____
_____
_____

Three beautiful things that I have noticed throughout my day:

_____
_____
_____
_____

~Embrace every possibility~

Date:_____

What I am grateful for:
_____
_____
_____
_____

What I have learned from my challenges:
_____
_____
_____
_____

Three things (big or small) that went well today:
_____
_____
_____
_____

Three beautiful things that I have noticed throughout my day:
_____
_____
_____
_____

~Enjoy the journey~

Date:_____

What I am grateful for:
_____
_____
_____
_____

What I have learned from my challenges:
_____
_____
_____
_____

Three things (big or small) that went well today:
_____
_____
_____
_____

Three beautiful things that I have noticed throughout my day:
_____
_____
_____
_____

~Embrace every challenge~

Date:_____

What I am grateful for:

_____
_____
_____
_____

What I have learned from my challenges:

_____
_____
_____
_____

Three things (big or small) that went well today:

_____
_____
_____
_____

Three beautiful things that I have noticed throughout my day:

_____
_____
_____
_____

~Learn from every mistake~

Date:_____

What I am grateful for:

_____
_____
_____
_____

What I have learned from my challenges:

_____
_____
_____
_____

Three things (big or small) that went well today:

_____
_____
_____
_____

Three beautiful things that I have noticed throughout my day:

_____
_____
_____
_____

~You have all the power to change your life~

Date:_____

What I am grateful for:

_____
_____
_____
_____

What I have learned from my challenges:

_____
_____
_____
_____

Three things (big or small) that went well today:

_____
_____
_____
_____

Three beautiful things that I have noticed throughout my day:

_____
_____
_____
_____

~Focus on the positive, for whatever you think about grows~

Date:_____

What I am grateful for:

_____
_____
_____
_____

What I have learned from my challenges:

_____
_____
_____
_____

Three things (big or small) that went well today:

_____
_____
_____
_____

Three beautiful things that I have noticed throughout my day:

_____
_____
_____
_____

~Surround yourself with great people~

Date:_____

What I am grateful for:
_____
_____
_____
_____

What I have learned from my challenges:
_____
_____
_____
_____

Three things (big or small) that went well today:
_____
_____
_____
_____

Three beautiful things that I have noticed throughout my day:
_____
_____
_____
_____

~Be happy for no reason~

Date:_____

What I am grateful for:

_____
_____
_____
_____

What I have learned from my challenges:

_____
_____
_____
_____

Three things (big or small) that went well today:

_____
_____
_____
_____

Three beautiful things that I have noticed throughout my day:

_____
_____
_____
_____

~Enjoy this very moment, live in the now~

Date:_____

What I am grateful for:

_____
_____
_____
_____

What I have learned from my challenges:

_____
_____
_____
_____

Three things (big or small) that went well today:

_____
_____
_____
_____

Three beautiful things that I have noticed throughout my day:

_____
_____
_____
_____

~Optimism is the key to happiness~

Date:_____

What I am grateful for:

_____
_____
_____
_____

What I have learned from my challenges:

_____
_____
_____
_____

Three things (big or small) that went well today:

_____
_____
_____
_____

Three beautiful things that I have noticed throughout my day:

_____
_____
_____
_____

~Gratitude will allow you to become your true best self~

Date:_____

What I am grateful for:

_____
_____
_____
_____

What I have learned from my challenges:

_____
_____
_____
_____

Three things (big or small) that went well today:

_____
_____
_____
_____

Three beautiful things that I have noticed throughout my day:

_____
_____
_____
_____

~Be adaptable, accept change~

Date:_____

What I am grateful for:

_____
_____
_____
_____

What I have learned from my challenges:

_____
_____
_____
_____

Three things (big or small) that went well today:

_____
_____
_____
_____

Three beautiful things that I have noticed throughout my day:

_____
_____
_____
_____

~Be enthusiastic about life~

Date:_____

What I am grateful for:

_____
_____
_____
_____

What I have learned from my challenges:

_____
_____
_____
_____

Three things (big or small) that went well today:

_____
_____
_____
_____

Three beautiful things that I have noticed throughout my day:

_____
_____
_____
_____

~You are in control of your emotions, thus, your reality~

Date:_____

What I am grateful for:
_____
_____
_____
_____

What I have learned from my challenges:
_____
_____
_____
_____

Three things (big or small) that went well today:
_____
_____
_____
_____

Three beautiful things that I have noticed throughout my day:
_____
_____
_____
_____

~Celebrate your life and the good people in it~

Date:_____

What I am grateful for:
_____
_____
_____
_____

What I have learned from my challenges:
_____
_____
_____
_____

Three things (big or small) that went well today:
_____
_____
_____
_____

Three beautiful things that I have noticed throughout my day:
_____
_____
_____
_____

~Do things that make you feel content within~

Date:_____

What I am grateful for:

_____
_____
_____
_____

What I have learned from my challenges:

_____
_____
_____
_____

Three things (big or small) that went well today:

_____
_____
_____
_____

Three beautiful things that I have noticed throughout my day:

_____
_____
_____
_____

~Feed your soul with positivity~

My 30 Day Progression

My achievements in the last 30 days:

_____
_____
_____
_____
_____

How I perceive life differently today since the last 30 days:

_____
_____
_____
_____
_____

How I am more optimistic today since the last 30 days:

_____
_____
_____
_____
_____

What I have attracted into my life in the last 30 days:

_____
_____
_____
_____
_____

~Count your gains not your losses~

Date:_____

What I am grateful for:
_____
_____
_____
_____

What I have learned from my challenges:
_____
_____
_____
_____

Three things (big or small) that went well today:
_____
_____
_____
_____

Three beautiful things that I have noticed throughout my day:
_____
_____
_____
_____

~Everything that you experience is a reflection of what you feel inside~

Date:_____

What I am grateful for:

_____
_____
_____
_____

What I have learned from my challenges:

_____
_____
_____
_____

Three things (big or small) that went well today:

_____
_____
_____
_____

Three beautiful things that I have noticed throughout my day:

_____
_____
_____
_____

~Count your joys not your sorrows~

Date:_____

What I am grateful for:

_____
_____
_____
_____

What I have learned from my challenges:

_____
_____
_____
_____

Three things (big or small) that went well today:

_____
_____
_____
_____

Three beautiful things that I have noticed throughout my day:

_____
_____
_____
_____

~Start your days with a smile and laughter~

Date:_____

What I am grateful for:

_____
_____
_____
_____

What I have learned from my challenges:

_____
_____
_____
_____

Three things (big or small) that went well today:

_____
_____
_____
_____

Three beautiful things that I have noticed throughout my day:

_____
_____
_____
_____

~Make your life a growing experience, everything is a learning lesson~

Date:_____

What I am grateful for:

_____
_____
_____
_____

What I have learned from my challenges:

_____
_____
_____
_____

Three things (big or small) that went well today:

_____
_____
_____
_____

Three beautiful things that I have noticed throughout my day:

_____
_____
_____
_____

~The moment you realize that you have all the control, you reach a beautiful level of freedom~

Date:_____

What I am grateful for:

_____
_____
_____
_____

What I have learned from my challenges:

_____
_____
_____
_____

Three things (big or small) that went well today:

_____
_____
_____
_____

Three beautiful things that I have noticed throughout my day:

_____
_____
_____
_____

~Be gracious~

Date:_____

What I am grateful for:

_____
_____
_____
_____

What I have learned from my challenges:

_____
_____
_____
_____

Three things (big or small) that went well today:

_____
_____
_____
_____

Three beautiful things that I have noticed throughout my day:

_____
_____
_____
_____

~Invest in your inner self~

Date:_____

What I am grateful for:

_____
_____
_____
_____

What I have learned from my challenges:

_____
_____
_____
_____

Three things (big or small) that went well today:

_____
_____
_____
_____

Three beautiful things that I have noticed throughout my day:

_____
_____
_____
_____

~Today you get a second chance, use it wisely~

Date:_____

What I am grateful for:

_____
_____
_____
_____

What I have learned from my challenges:

_____
_____
_____
_____

Three things (big or small) that went well today:

_____
_____
_____
_____

Three beautiful things that I have noticed throughout my day:

_____
_____
_____
_____

~Inhale the positive, exhale the negative~

Date:_____

What I am grateful for:
_____
_____
_____
_____

What I have learned from my challenges:
_____
_____
_____
_____

Three things (big or small) that went well today:
_____
_____
_____
_____

Three beautiful things that I have noticed throughout my day:
_____
_____
_____
_____

~Never take life or people for granted~

Date:_____

What I am grateful for:
_____
_____
_____
_____

What I have learned from my challenges:
_____
_____
_____
_____

Three things (big or small) that went well today:
_____
_____
_____
_____

Three beautiful things that I have noticed throughout my day:
_____
_____
_____
_____

~Don't make excuses, make changes~

Date:_____

What I am grateful for:

_____
_____
_____
_____

What I have learned from my challenges:

_____
_____
_____
_____

Three things (big or small) that went well today:

_____
_____
_____
_____

Three beautiful things that I have noticed throughout my day:

_____
_____
_____
_____

~Create peace and harmony~

Date:_____

What I am grateful for:
_____
_____
_____
_____

What I have learned from my challenges:
_____
_____
_____
_____

Three things (big or small) that went well today:
_____
_____
_____
_____

Three beautiful things that I have noticed throughout my day:
_____
_____
_____
_____

~Today is a fresh start, what will you make of it?~

Date:_____

What I am grateful for:

_____
_____
_____
_____

What I have learned from my challenges:

_____
_____
_____
_____

Three things (big or small) that went well today:

_____
_____
_____
_____

Three beautiful things that I have noticed throughout my day:

_____
_____
_____
_____

~Be uplifting~

Date:_____

What I am grateful for:

_____
_____
_____
_____

What I have learned from my challenges:

_____
_____
_____
_____

Three things (big or small) that went well today:

_____
_____
_____
_____

Three beautiful things that I have noticed throughout my day:

_____
_____
_____
_____

~Have faith, be strong and enjoy the journey~

Date:_____

What I am grateful for:

_____
_____
_____
_____

What I have learned from my challenges:

_____
_____
_____
_____

Three things (big or small) that went well today:

_____
_____
_____
_____

Three beautiful things that I have noticed throughout my day:

_____
_____
_____
_____

~This is your life, live it your way~

Date:_____

What I am grateful for:

_____
_____
_____
_____

What I have learned from my challenges:

_____
_____
_____
_____

Three things (big or small) that went well today:

_____
_____
_____
_____

Three beautiful things that I have noticed throughout my day:

_____
_____
_____
_____

~Sit in silence and you will discover much~

Date:_____

What I am grateful for:

_____
_____
_____
_____

What I have learned from my challenges:

_____
_____
_____
_____

Three things (big or small) that went well today:

_____
_____
_____
_____

Three beautiful things that I have noticed throughout my day:

_____
_____
_____
_____

~Change your thoughts, change your words, change your story~

Date:_____

What I am grateful for:

_____
_____
_____
_____

What I have learned from my challenges:

_____
_____
_____
_____

Three things (big or small) that went well today:

_____
_____
_____
_____

Three beautiful things that I have noticed throughout my day:

_____
_____
_____
_____

~You are love and you are light~

Date:_____

What I am grateful for:

_____
_____
_____
_____

What I have learned from my challenges:

_____
_____
_____
_____

Three things (big or small) that went well today:

_____
_____
_____
_____

Three beautiful things that I have noticed throughout my day:

_____
_____
_____
_____

~When we are grateful for what we have, we are ready to receive more~

Date:_____

What I am grateful for:
_____
_____
_____
_____

What I have learned from my challenges:
_____
_____
_____
_____

Three things (big or small) that went well today:
_____
_____
_____
_____

Three beautiful things that I have noticed throughout my day:
_____
_____
_____
_____

~The mind is very powerful, what you think, you will become~

Date:_____

What I am grateful for:

_____
_____
_____
_____

What I have learned from my challenges:

_____
_____
_____
_____

Three things (big or small) that went well today:

_____
_____
_____
_____

Three beautiful things that I have noticed throughout my day:

_____
_____
_____
_____

~Be grateful for everything that you have and have accomplished~

Date:_____

What I am grateful for:

_____
_____
_____
_____

What I have learned from my challenges:

_____
_____
_____
_____

Three things (big or small) that went well today:

_____
_____
_____
_____

Three beautiful things that I have noticed throughout my day:

_____
_____
_____
_____

~Words are very powerful, they shape our reality~

Date:_____

What I am grateful for:

_____
_____
_____
_____

What I have learned from my challenges:

_____
_____
_____
_____

Three things (big or small) that went well today:

_____
_____
_____
_____

Three beautiful things that I have noticed throughout my day:

_____
_____
_____
_____

~Have a vision, focus, stay on your path and keep going until you reach your destination~

Date:_____

What I am grateful for:

_____
_____
_____
_____

What I have learned from my challenges:

_____
_____
_____
_____

Three things (big or small) that went well today:

_____
_____
_____
_____

Three beautiful things that I have noticed throughout my day:

_____
_____
_____
_____

~Life is full of opportunities and possibilities~

Date:_____

What I am grateful for:

_____
_____
_____
_____

What I have learned from my challenges:

_____
_____
_____
_____

Three things (big or small) that went well today:

_____
_____
_____
_____

Three beautiful things that I have noticed throughout my day:

_____
_____
_____
_____

~You could never experience true happiness if you are not grateful for what you already have~

Date:_____

What I am grateful for:

_____
_____
_____
_____

What I have learned from my challenges:

_____
_____
_____
_____

Three things (big or small) that went well today:

_____
_____
_____
_____

Three beautiful things that I have noticed throughout my day:

_____
_____
_____
_____

~Make the decision to be the greatest version of yourself, who you become is all in your hands~

Date:_____

What I am grateful for:

_____
_____
_____
_____

What I have learned from my challenges:

_____
_____
_____
_____

Three things (big or small) that went well today:

_____
_____
_____
_____

Three beautiful things that I have noticed throughout my day:

_____
_____
_____
_____

~Don't wait to tell someone you love and appreciate them~

Date:_____

What I am grateful for:

_____
_____
_____
_____

What I have learned from my challenges:

_____
_____
_____
_____

Three things (big or small) that went well today:

_____
_____
_____
_____

Three beautiful things that I have noticed throughout my day:

_____
_____
_____
_____

~Say thank you to those who have hurt you, for they are your greatest teachers~

Date:_____

What I am grateful for:

_____
_____
_____
_____

What I have learned from my challenges:

_____
_____
_____
_____

Three things (big or small) that went well today:

_____
_____
_____
_____

Three beautiful things that I have noticed throughout my day:

_____
_____
_____
_____

~Every single day is a blessing~

My 30 Day Progression

My achievements in the last 30 days:

_____
_____
_____
_____
_____

How I perceive life differently today since the last 30 days:

_____
_____
_____
_____
_____

How I am more optimistic today since the last 30 days:

_____
_____
_____
_____
_____

What I have attracted into my life in the last 30 days:

_____
_____
_____
_____
_____

~You deserve only the best that life has to offer~

Date:_____

What I am grateful for:

_____
_____
_____
_____

What I have learned from my challenges:

_____
_____
_____
_____

Three things (big or small) that went well today:

_____
_____
_____
_____

Three beautiful things that I have noticed throughout my day:

_____
_____
_____
_____

~Give without the intention of receiving~

Date:_____

What I am grateful for:
_____
_____
_____
_____

What I have learned from my challenges:
_____
_____
_____
_____

Three things (big or small) that went well today:
_____
_____
_____
_____

Three beautiful things that I have noticed throughout my day:
_____
_____
_____
_____

~Appreciate all that you already have in your life~

Date:_____

What I am grateful for:
_____
_____
_____
_____

What I have learned from my challenges:
_____
_____
_____
_____

Three things (big or small) that went well today:
_____
_____
_____
_____

Three beautiful things that I have noticed throughout my day:
_____
_____
_____
_____

~Take charge of your thoughts, your mind, your life~

Date:_____

What I am grateful for:

_____
_____
_____
_____

What I have learned from my challenges:

_____
_____
_____
_____

Three things (big or small) that went well today:

_____
_____
_____
_____

Three beautiful things that I have noticed throughout my day:

_____
_____
_____
_____

~A smile can change your whole day~

Date:_____

What I am grateful for:

_____
_____
_____
_____

What I have learned from my challenges:

_____
_____
_____
_____

Three things (big or small) that went well today:

_____
_____
_____
_____

Three beautiful things that I have noticed throughout my day:

_____
_____
_____
_____

~Count your blessings and prepare to receive more~

Date:_____

What I am grateful for:

_____
_____
_____
_____

What I have learned from my challenges:

_____
_____
_____
_____

Three things (big or small) that went well today:

_____
_____
_____
_____

Three beautiful things that I have noticed throughout my day:

_____
_____
_____
_____

~Surround yourself with happy, successful people and you will be a happy, successful person~

Date:_____

What I am grateful for:

_____

_____

_____

_____

What I have learned from my challenges:

_____

_____

_____

_____

Three things (big or small) that went well today:

_____

_____

_____

_____

Three beautiful things that I have noticed throughout my day:

_____

_____

_____

_____

~Set a good example for others to follow~

Date:_____

What I am grateful for:

_____
_____
_____
_____

What I have learned from my challenges:

_____
_____
_____
_____

Three things (big or small) that went well today:

_____
_____
_____
_____

Three beautiful things that I have noticed throughout my day:

_____
_____
_____
_____

~Laughter is healing~

Date:_____

What I am grateful for:

_____
_____
_____
_____

What I have learned from my challenges:

_____
_____
_____
_____

Three things (big or small) that went well today:

_____
_____
_____
_____

Three beautiful things that I have noticed throughout my day:

_____
_____
_____
_____

~Get ready to take control of your life and smile while you're at it~

Date:_____

What I am grateful for:

_____
_____
_____
_____

What I have learned from my challenges:

_____
_____
_____
_____

Three things (big or small) that went well today:

_____
_____
_____
_____

Three beautiful things that I have noticed throughout my day:

_____
_____
_____
_____

~There's something special about you~

Date:_____

What I am grateful for:

_____
_____
_____
_____

What I have learned from my challenges:

_____
_____
_____
_____

Three things (big or small) that went well today:

_____
_____
_____
_____

Three beautiful things that I have noticed throughout my day:

_____
_____
_____
_____

~A kind gesture can change someone's whole life~

Date:_____

What I am grateful for:

_____
_____
_____
_____

What I have learned from my challenges:

_____
_____
_____
_____

Three things (big or small) that went well today:

_____
_____
_____
_____

Three beautiful things that I have noticed throughout my day:

_____
_____
_____
_____

~Make personal growth a part of your everyday life~

Date:_____

What I am grateful for:

_____
_____
_____
_____

What I have learned from my challenges:

_____
_____
_____
_____

Three things (big or small) that went well today:

_____
_____
_____
_____

Three beautiful things that I have noticed throughout my day:

_____
_____
_____
_____

~Envision a white shield around you and only let in positivity~

Date:_____

What I am grateful for:
_____
_____
_____
_____

What I have learned from my challenges:
_____
_____
_____
_____

Three things (big or small) that went well today:
_____
_____
_____
_____

Three beautiful things that I have noticed throughout my day:
_____
_____
_____
_____

~Courage and change leads to freedom~

Date:_____

What I am grateful for:

_____
_____
_____
_____

What I have learned from my challenges:

_____
_____
_____
_____

Three things (big or small) that went well today:

_____
_____
_____
_____

Three beautiful things that I have noticed throughout my day:

_____
_____
_____
_____

~Do five minutes minimum of deep breathing everyday~

Date:_____

What I am grateful for:

_____
_____
_____
_____

What I have learned from my challenges:

_____
_____
_____
_____

Three things (big or small) that went well today:

_____
_____
_____
_____

Three beautiful things that I have noticed throughout my day:

_____
_____
_____
_____

~Find the lesson in every challenge~

Date:_____

What I am grateful for:

_____
_____
_____
_____

What I have learned from my challenges:

_____
_____
_____
_____

Three things (big or small) that went well today:

_____
_____
_____
_____

Three beautiful things that I have noticed throughout my day:

_____
_____
_____
_____

~Be loyal, kind and generous and you will receive loyalty, kindness and generosity in return~

Date:_____

What I am grateful for:
_____
_____
_____
_____

What I have learned from my challenges:
_____
_____
_____
_____

Three things (big or small) that went well today:
_____
_____
_____
_____

Three beautiful things that I have noticed throughout my day:
_____
_____
_____
_____

~Life is what you make of it, make the best of it~

Date:_____

What I am grateful for:

_____
_____
_____
_____

What I have learned from my challenges:

_____
_____
_____
_____

Three things (big or small) that went well today:

_____
_____
_____
_____

Three beautiful things that I have noticed throughout my day:

_____
_____
_____
_____

~Live like children do, live in the moment~

Date:_____

What I am grateful for:

_____
_____
_____
_____

What I have learned from my challenges:

_____
_____
_____
_____

Three things (big or small) that went well today:

_____
_____
_____
_____

Three beautiful things that I have noticed throughout my day:

_____
_____
_____
_____

~It's no coincidence that rainbows come after a storm~

Date:_____

What I am grateful for:
_____
_____
_____
_____

What I have learned from my challenges:
_____
_____
_____
_____

Three things (big or small) that went well today:
_____
_____
_____
_____

Three beautiful things that I have noticed throughout my day:
_____
_____
_____
_____

~You must have an inner vision in order to create an outer experience~

Date:_____

What I am grateful for:
_____
_____
_____
_____

What I have learned from my challenges:
_____
_____
_____
_____

Three things (big or small) that went well today:
_____
_____
_____
_____

Three beautiful things that I have noticed throughout my day:
_____
_____
_____
_____

~A person who experiences life their way, will see things no one has ever seen before~

Date:_____

What I am grateful for:

_____
_____
_____
_____

What I have learned from my challenges:

_____
_____
_____
_____

Three things (big or small) that went well today:

_____
_____
_____
_____

Three beautiful things that I have noticed throughout my day:

_____
_____
_____
_____

~Speak the truth, speak your truth~

Date:_____

What I am grateful for:

_____
_____
_____
_____

What I have learned from my challenges:

_____
_____
_____
_____

Three things (big or small) that went well today:

_____
_____
_____
_____

Three beautiful things that I have noticed throughout my day:

_____
_____
_____
_____

~Everything that you currently have, is a reflection of what you once believed~

Date:_____

What I am grateful for:

_____
_____
_____
_____

What I have learned from my challenges:

_____
_____
_____
_____

Three things (big or small) that went well today:

_____
_____
_____
_____

Three beautiful things that I have noticed throughout my day:

_____
_____
_____
_____

~Live with purpose, live with love~

Date:_____

What I am grateful for:

_____
_____
_____
_____

What I have learned from my challenges:

_____
_____
_____
_____

Three things (big or small) that went well today:

_____
_____
_____
_____

Three beautiful things that I have noticed throughout my day:

_____
_____
_____
_____

~Everyone's perception of reality differs, don't let someone else's reality diminish yours~

Date:_____

What I am grateful for:
_____
_____
_____
_____

What I have learned from my challenges:
_____
_____
_____
_____

Three things (big or small) that went well today:
_____
_____
_____
_____

Three beautiful things that I have noticed throughout my day:
_____
_____
_____
_____

~Take a moment everyday to just go deep within yourself~

Date:_____

What I am grateful for:

_____
_____
_____
_____

What I have learned from my challenges:

_____
_____
_____
_____

Three things (big or small) that went well today:

_____
_____
_____
_____

Three beautiful things that I have noticed throughout my day:

_____
_____
_____
_____

~Know that you already are greatness, it is not something that you are destined to become~

Date:_____

What I am grateful for:
_____
_____
_____
_____

What I have learned from my challenges:
_____
_____
_____
_____

Three things (big or small) that went well today:
_____
_____
_____
_____

Three beautiful things that I have noticed throughout my day:
_____
_____
_____
_____

~Turn your wounds into scars, turn your scars into wisdom~

Date:_____

What I am grateful for:

_____
_____
_____
_____

What I have learned from my challenges:

_____
_____
_____
_____

Three things (big or small) that went well today:

_____
_____
_____
_____

Three beautiful things that I have noticed throughout my day:

_____
_____
_____
_____

~Do good regardless if people will know you did it or not~

My 30 Day Progression

My achievements in the last 30 days:

_____
_____
_____
_____
_____

How I perceive life differently today since the last 30 days:

_____
_____
_____
_____
_____

How I am more optimistic today since the last 30 days:

_____
_____
_____
_____
_____

What I have attracted into my life in the last 30 days:

_____
_____
_____
_____
_____

~Every time you reach a milestone toward success, you have nowhere else to go but up~

Date:_____

What I am grateful for:

_____
_____
_____
_____

What I have learned from my challenges:

_____
_____
_____
_____

Three things (big or small) that went well today:

_____
_____
_____
_____

Three beautiful things that I have noticed throughout my day:

_____
_____
_____
_____

~It's not where you come from that determines where you'll end up~

Date:_____

What I am grateful for:

_____
_____
_____
_____

What I have learned from my challenges:

_____
_____
_____
_____

Three things (big or small) that went well today:

_____
_____
_____
_____

Three beautiful things that I have noticed throughout my day:

_____
_____
_____
_____

~Don't rush through life, savour every moment~

Date:_____

What I am grateful for:

_____
_____
_____
_____

What I have learned from my challenges:

_____
_____
_____
_____

Three things (big or small) that went well today:

_____
_____
_____
_____

Three beautiful things that I have noticed throughout my day:

_____
_____
_____
_____

~Be grateful for every blessing, every mistake, every laugh, every tear, for they have made you who you are today~

Date:_____

What I am grateful for:

_____
_____
_____
_____

What I have learned from my challenges:

_____
_____
_____
_____

Three things (big or small) that went well today:

_____
_____
_____
_____

Three beautiful things that I have noticed throughout my day:

_____
_____
_____
_____

~You can't live a positive life with a negative mind~

Date:_____

What I am grateful for:

_____
_____
_____
_____

What I have learned from my challenges:

_____
_____
_____
_____

Three things (big or small) that went well today:

_____
_____
_____
_____

Three beautiful things that I have noticed throughout my day:

_____
_____
_____
_____

~Live everyday like it's your very last~

Date:_____

What I am grateful for:

_____
_____
_____
_____

What I have learned from my challenges:

_____
_____
_____
_____

Three things (big or small) that went well today:

_____
_____
_____
_____

Three beautiful things that I have noticed throughout my day:

_____
_____
_____
_____

~You could not appreciate love without having experienced pain~

Date:_____

What I am grateful for:

_____
_____
_____
_____

What I have learned from my challenges:

_____
_____
_____
_____

Three things (big or small) that went well today:

_____
_____
_____
_____

Three beautiful things that I have noticed throughout my day:

_____
_____
_____
_____

~An inch today, becomes a mile tomorrow, it all adds up, so get started~

Date:_____

What I am grateful for:

_____
_____
_____
_____

What I have learned from my challenges:

_____
_____
_____
_____

Three things (big or small) that went well today:

_____
_____
_____
_____

Three beautiful things that I have noticed throughout my day:

_____
_____
_____
_____

~Think like children do, they are non judgemental, full of imagination and possibilities~

Date:_____

What I am grateful for:

_____
_____
_____
_____

What I have learned from my challenges:

_____
_____
_____
_____

Three things (big or small) that went well today:

_____
_____
_____
_____

Three beautiful things that I have noticed throughout my day:

_____
_____
_____
_____

~At times, you might experience destruction but never allow yourself to be destroyed~

Date:_____

What I am grateful for:

_____
_____
_____
_____

What I have learned from my challenges:

_____
_____
_____
_____

Three things (big or small) that went well today:

_____
_____
_____
_____

Three beautiful things that I have noticed throughout my day:

_____
_____
_____
_____

~Life is about believing in yourself and helping others to do the same~

Date:_____

What I am grateful for:

_____
_____
_____
_____

What I have learned from my challenges:

_____
_____
_____
_____

Three things (big or small) that went well today:

_____
_____
_____
_____

Three beautiful things that I have noticed throughout my day:

_____
_____
_____
_____

~Everybody has something special that someone else needs~

Date:_____

What I am grateful for:

_____
_____
_____
_____

What I have learned from my challenges:

_____
_____
_____
_____

Three things (big or small) that went well today:

_____
_____
_____
_____

Three beautiful things that I have noticed throughout my day:

_____
_____
_____
_____

~Go out there and manifest whatever it is that you want~

Date:_____

What I am grateful for:

_____
_____
_____
_____

What I have learned from my challenges:

_____
_____
_____
_____

Three things (big or small) that went well today:

_____
_____
_____
_____

Three beautiful things that I have noticed throughout my day:

_____
_____
_____
_____

~Stop re-reading the last chapter of your life and start a new one~

Date:_____

What I am grateful for:

_____
_____
_____
_____

What I have learned from my challenges:

_____
_____
_____
_____

Three things (big or small) that went well today:

_____
_____
_____
_____

Three beautiful things that I have noticed throughout my day:

_____
_____
_____
_____

~When you compare yourself to others, you are robbing yourself of who you are~

Date:_____

What I am grateful for:

_____
_____
_____
_____

What I have learned from my challenges:

_____
_____
_____
_____

Three things (big or small) that went well today:

_____
_____
_____
_____

Three beautiful things that I have noticed throughout my day:

_____
_____
_____
_____

~Imperfect action is better than no action at all~

Date:_____

What I am grateful for:

_____
_____
_____
_____

What I have learned from my challenges:

_____
_____
_____
_____

Three things (big or small) that went well today:

_____
_____
_____
_____

Three beautiful things that I have noticed throughout my day:

_____
_____
_____
_____

~You are a phenomenal person~

Date:_____

What I am grateful for:

_____
_____
_____
_____

What I have learned from my challenges:

_____
_____
_____
_____

Three things (big or small) that went well today:

_____
_____
_____
_____

Three beautiful things that I have noticed throughout my day:

_____
_____
_____
_____

~Trust yourself, you have all the answers~

Date:_____

What I am grateful for:

_____
_____
_____
_____

What I have learned from my challenges:

_____
_____
_____
_____

Three things (big or small) that went well today:

_____
_____
_____
_____

Three beautiful things that I have noticed throughout my day:

_____
_____
_____
_____

~Be willing to step out of your comfort zone~

Date:_____

What I am grateful for:

_____
_____
_____
_____

What I have learned from my challenges:

_____
_____
_____
_____

Three things (big or small) that went well today:

_____
_____
_____
_____

Three beautiful things that I have noticed throughout my day:

_____
_____
_____
_____

~Make a life before you make a living~

Date:_____

What I am grateful for:

_____
_____
_____
_____

What I have learned from my challenges:

_____
_____
_____
_____

Three things (big or small) that went well today:

_____
_____
_____
_____

Three beautiful things that I have noticed throughout my day:

_____
_____
_____
_____

~Only strive for excellence~

Date:_____

What I am grateful for:
_____
_____
_____
_____

What I have learned from my challenges:
_____
_____
_____
_____

Three things (big or small) that went well today:
_____
_____
_____
_____

Three beautiful things that I have noticed throughout my day:
_____
_____
_____
_____

~Be someone who radiates joy, positivity, love~

Date:_____

What I am grateful for:

_____
_____
_____
_____

What I have learned from my challenges:

_____
_____
_____
_____

Three things (big or small) that went well today:

_____
_____
_____
_____

Three beautiful things that I have noticed throughout my day:

_____
_____
_____
_____

~If you don't understand failure, you could never understand achievement~

Date:_____

What I am grateful for:

_____
_____
_____
_____

What I have learned from my challenges:

_____
_____
_____
_____

Three things (big or small) that went well today:

_____
_____
_____
_____

Three beautiful things that I have noticed throughout my day:

_____
_____
_____
_____

~You never really start over, you always start right from where you are~

Date:_____

What I am grateful for:

_____
_____
_____
_____

What I have learned from my challenges:

_____
_____
_____
_____

Three things (big or small) that went well today:

_____
_____
_____
_____

Three beautiful things that I have noticed throughout my day:

_____
_____
_____
_____

~If you're searching for true love, you first need to learn to truly love yourself~

Date:_____

What I am grateful for:

_____
_____
_____
_____

What I have learned from my challenges:

_____
_____
_____
_____

Three things (big or small) that went well today:

_____
_____
_____
_____

Three beautiful things that I have noticed throughout my day:

_____
_____
_____
_____

~You alone are enough~

Date:_____

What I am grateful for:

_____
_____
_____
_____

What I have learned from my challenges:

_____
_____
_____
_____

Three things (big or small) that went well today:

_____
_____
_____
_____

Three beautiful things that I have noticed throughout my day:

_____
_____
_____
_____

~If you never encounter fear, you could never understand courage~

Date:_____

What I am grateful for:

_____
_____
_____
_____

What I have learned from my challenges:

_____
_____
_____
_____

Three things (big or small) that went well today:

_____
_____
_____
_____

Three beautiful things that I have noticed throughout my day:

_____
_____
_____
_____

~Be good to yourself and those around you~

Date:_____

What I am grateful for:

_____
_____
_____
_____

What I have learned from my challenges:

_____
_____
_____
_____

Three things (big or small) that went well today:

_____
_____
_____
_____

Three beautiful things that I have noticed throughout my day:

_____
_____
_____
_____

~Don't focus on the loss, focus on the memory~

Date:_____

What I am grateful for:

_____
_____
_____
_____

What I have learned from my challenges:

_____
_____
_____
_____

Three things (big or small) that went well today:

_____
_____
_____
_____

Three beautiful things that I have noticed throughout my day:

_____
_____
_____
_____

~Do what everyone else thinks is impossible~

Date:_____

What I am grateful for:

_____
_____
_____
_____

What I have learned from my challenges:

_____
_____
_____
_____

Three things (big or small) that went well today:

_____
_____
_____
_____

Three beautiful things that I have noticed throughout my day:

_____
_____
_____
_____

~If you want to see a change in the world let it start with you~

My 30 Day Progression

My achievements in the last 30 days:

_____
_____
_____
_____
_____

How I perceive life differently today since the last 30 days:

_____
_____
_____
_____
_____

How I am more optimistic today since the last 30 days:

_____
_____
_____
_____
_____

What I have attracted into my life in the last 30 days:

_____
_____
_____
_____
_____

~When you focus on what you don't want, you are missing the point~

Date:_____

What I am grateful for:

_____
_____
_____
_____

What I have learned from my challenges:

_____
_____
_____
_____

Three things (big or small) that went well today:

_____
_____
_____
_____

Three beautiful things that I have noticed throughout my day:

_____
_____
_____
_____

~You are in charge of your emotions, choose happiness~

Date:_____

What I am grateful for:

_____
_____
_____
_____

What I have learned from my challenges:

_____
_____
_____
_____

Three things (big or small) that went well today:

_____
_____
_____
_____

Three beautiful things that I have noticed throughout my day:

_____
_____
_____
_____

~Break the habit of talking about your problems and talk about your joys instead~

Date:_____

What I am grateful for:

_____
_____
_____
_____

What I have learned from my challenges:

_____
_____
_____
_____

Three things (big or small) that went well today:

_____
_____
_____
_____

Three beautiful things that I have noticed throughout my day:

_____
_____
_____
_____

~Failure is not the outcome, failure is never having tried~

Date:_____

What I am grateful for:

_____
_____
_____
_____

What I have learned from my challenges:

_____
_____
_____
_____

Three things (big or small) that went well today:

_____
_____
_____
_____

Three beautiful things that I have noticed throughout my day:

_____
_____
_____
_____

~Dream it, get inspired, take action and achieve it~

Date:_____

What I am grateful for:

_____
_____
_____
_____

What I have learned from my challenges:

_____
_____
_____
_____

Three things (big or small) that went well today:

_____
_____
_____
_____

Three beautiful things that I have noticed throughout my day:

_____
_____
_____
_____

~Healthy minds attract healthy people~

Date:_____

What I am grateful for:

_____
_____
_____
_____

What I have learned from my challenges:

_____
_____
_____
_____

Three things (big or small) that went well today:

_____
_____
_____
_____

Three beautiful things that I have noticed throughout my day:

_____
_____
_____
_____

~Be like the sun, rise no matter what happens~

Date:_____

What I am grateful for:

_____
_____
_____
_____

What I have learned from my challenges:

_____
_____
_____
_____

Three things (big or small) that went well today:

_____
_____
_____
_____

Three beautiful things that I have noticed throughout my day:

_____
_____
_____
_____

~Do something that motivates you every single day~

Date:_____

What I am grateful for:

_____
_____
_____
_____

What I have learned from my challenges:

_____
_____
_____
_____

Three things (big or small) that went well today:

_____
_____
_____
_____

Three beautiful things that I have noticed throughout my day:

_____
_____
_____
_____

~Optimism will set you free~

Date:_____

What I am grateful for:

_____
_____
_____
_____

What I have learned from my challenges:

_____
_____
_____
_____

Three things (big or small) that went well today:

_____
_____
_____
_____

Three beautiful things that I have noticed throughout my day:

_____
_____
_____
_____

~Train yourself to find the beauty in everything~

Date:_____

What I am grateful for:

_____
_____
_____
_____

What I have learned from my challenges:

_____
_____
_____
_____

Three things (big or small) that went well today:

_____
_____
_____
_____

Three beautiful things that I have noticed throughout my day:

_____
_____
_____
_____

~Everything that exists was once nonexistent, what will you create?~

Date:_____

What I am grateful for:

_____
_____
_____
_____

What I have learned from my challenges:

_____
_____
_____
_____

Three things (big or small) that went well today:

_____
_____
_____
_____

Three beautiful things that I have noticed throughout my day:

_____
_____
_____
_____

~You have all the power you need within you~

Date:_____

What I am grateful for:

_____
_____
_____
_____

What I have learned from my challenges:

_____
_____
_____
_____

Three things (big or small) that went well today:

_____
_____
_____
_____

Three beautiful things that I have noticed throughout my day:

_____
_____
_____
_____

~Focus on what it is you truly want, then make it happen~

Date:_____

What I am grateful for:

_____
_____
_____
_____

What I have learned from my challenges:

_____
_____
_____
_____

Three things (big or small) that went well today:

_____
_____
_____
_____

Three beautiful things that I have noticed throughout my day:

_____
_____
_____
_____

~You need to believe in yourself before someone else can believe in you~

Date:_____

What I am grateful for:

_____
_____
_____
_____

What I have learned from my challenges:

_____
_____
_____
_____

Three things (big or small) that went well today:

_____
_____
_____
_____

Three beautiful things that I have noticed throughout my day:

_____
_____
_____
_____

~They can laugh, they can judge or they can follow you but they cannot stop you~

Date:_____

What I am grateful for:

_____
_____
_____
_____

What I have learned from my challenges:

_____
_____
_____
_____

Three things (big or small) that went well today:

_____
_____
_____
_____

Three beautiful things that I have noticed throughout my day:

_____
_____
_____
_____

~Have faith, what you desire is in the works~

Date:_____

What I am grateful for:

_____
_____
_____
_____

What I have learned from my challenges:

_____
_____
_____
_____

Three things (big or small) that went well today:

_____
_____
_____
_____

Three beautiful things that I have noticed throughout my day:

_____
_____
_____
_____

~Do more of what makes you happy~

Date:_____

What I am grateful for:

_____
_____
_____
_____

What I have learned from my challenges:

_____
_____
_____
_____

Three things (big or small) that went well today:

_____
_____
_____
_____

Three beautiful things that I have noticed throughout my day:

_____
_____
_____
_____

~Go with the wind, dance in the rain and charge through every storm~

Date:_____

What I am grateful for:

_____
_____
_____
_____

What I have learned from my challenges:

_____
_____
_____
_____

Three things (big or small) that went well today:

_____
_____
_____
_____

Three beautiful things that I have noticed throughout my day:

_____
_____
_____
_____

~Fall in love with you first, no one can do that before you do~

Date:_____

What I am grateful for:

_____
_____
_____
_____

What I have learned from my challenges:

_____
_____
_____
_____

Three things (big or small) that went well today:

_____
_____
_____
_____

Three beautiful things that I have noticed throughout my day:

_____
_____
_____
_____

~Be happy with what you have, there are others who are grateful with less than you~

Date:_____

What I am grateful for:

_____
_____
_____
_____

What I have learned from my challenges:

_____
_____
_____
_____

Three things (big or small) that went well today:

_____
_____
_____
_____

Three beautiful things that I have noticed throughout my day:

_____
_____
_____
_____

~When you are optimistic, you automatically put yourself in a state of joy~

Date:_____

What I am grateful for:

_____
_____
_____
_____

What I have learned from my challenges:

_____
_____
_____
_____

Three things (big or small) that went well today:

_____
_____
_____
_____

Three beautiful things that I have noticed throughout my day:

_____
_____
_____
_____

~Be happy just for being you~

Date:_____

What I am grateful for:

_____
_____
_____
_____

What I have learned from my challenges:

_____
_____
_____
_____

Three things (big or small) that went well today:

_____
_____
_____
_____

Three beautiful things that I have noticed throughout my day:

_____
_____
_____
_____

~Wish good upon everyone because what you put out there, you will attract~

Date:_____

What I am grateful for:

_____
_____
_____
_____

What I have learned from my challenges:

_____
_____
_____
_____

Three things (big or small) that went well today:

_____
_____
_____
_____

Three beautiful things that I have noticed throughout my day:

_____
_____
_____
_____

~Don't depend on someone else to make you happy~

Date:_____

What I am grateful for:

_____
_____
_____
_____

What I have learned from my challenges:

_____
_____
_____
_____

Three things (big or small) that went well today:

_____
_____
_____
_____

Three beautiful things that I have noticed throughout my day:

_____
_____
_____
_____

~Happiness and satisfaction could never come to those who are not grateful for what they already have~

Date:_____

What I am grateful for:

_____
_____
_____
_____

What I have learned from my challenges:

_____
_____
_____
_____

Three things (big or small) that went well today:

_____
_____
_____
_____

Three beautiful things that I have noticed throughout my day:

_____
_____
_____
_____

~Do a good gesture for someone and ask them to repeat the gesture of kindness for someone else~

Date:_____

What I am grateful for:

_____
_____
_____
_____

What I have learned from my challenges:

_____
_____
_____
_____

Three things (big or small) that went well today:

_____
_____
_____
_____

Three beautiful things that I have noticed throughout my day:

_____
_____
_____
_____

~Love is all you need~

Date:_____

What I am grateful for:

_____
_____
_____
_____

What I have learned from my challenges:

_____
_____
_____
_____

Three things (big or small) that went well today:

_____
_____
_____
_____

Three beautiful things that I have noticed throughout my day:

_____
_____
_____
_____

~Sometimes we need to do things other people would never do, in order to lead a life others can only dream of~

Date:_____

What I am grateful for:

_____
_____
_____
_____

What I have learned from my challenges:

_____
_____
_____
_____

Three things (big or small) that went well today:

_____
_____
_____
_____

Three beautiful things that I have noticed throughout my day:

_____
_____
_____
_____

~Do things that will inspire other people~

Date:_____

What I am grateful for:

_____
_____
_____
_____

What I have learned from my challenges:

_____
_____
_____
_____

Three things (big or small) that went well today:

_____
_____
_____
_____

Three beautiful things that I have noticed throughout my day:

_____
_____
_____
_____

~When you are positive, doors will open for you~

Date:_____

What I am grateful for:

_____
_____
_____
_____

What I have learned from my challenges:

_____
_____
_____
_____

Three things (big or small) that went well today:

_____
_____
_____
_____

Three beautiful things that I have noticed throughout my day:

_____
_____
_____
_____

~There's always a light at the end of a dark tunnel~

My 30 Day Progression

My achievements in the last 30 days:

_____
_____
_____
_____
_____

How I perceive life differently today since the last 30 days:

_____
_____
_____
_____
_____

How I am more optimistic today since the last 30 days:

_____
_____
_____
_____
_____

What I have attracted into my life in the last 30 days:

_____
_____
_____
_____
_____

~Sometimes you don't need to know where you're going, as long as you're moving forward~

Date:_____

What I am grateful for:

_____
_____
_____
_____

What I have learned from my challenges:

_____
_____
_____
_____

Three things (big or small) that went well today:

_____
_____
_____
_____

Three beautiful things that I have noticed throughout my day:

_____
_____
_____
_____

~Celebrate your life every single day~

Date:_____

What I am grateful for:

_____
_____
_____
_____

What I have learned from my challenges:

_____
_____
_____
_____

Three things (big or small) that went well today:

_____
_____
_____
_____

Three beautiful things that I have noticed throughout my day:

_____
_____
_____
_____

~Follow your heart and miracles will happen~

Date:_____

What I am grateful for:

_____
_____
_____
_____

What I have learned from my challenges:

_____
_____
_____
_____

Three things (big or small) that went well today:

_____
_____
_____
_____

Three beautiful things that I have noticed throughout my day:

_____
_____
_____
_____

~A sure way to know where you're headed in life, is to figure out what you are thinking~

Date:_____

What I am grateful for:

_____
_____
_____
_____

What I have learned from my challenges:

_____
_____
_____
_____

Three things (big or small) that went well today:

_____
_____
_____
_____

Three beautiful things that I have noticed throughout my day:

_____
_____
_____
_____

~Happiness is a conscious choice, if you decide you want it, then you can have it~

Date:_____

What I am grateful for:

_____
_____
_____
_____

What I have learned from my challenges:

_____
_____
_____
_____

Three things (big or small) that went well today:

_____
_____
_____
_____

Three beautiful things that I have noticed throughout my day:

_____
_____
_____
_____

~Forgive yourself for having believed in the past that you weren't good enough, because you alone are enough~

Date:_____

What I am grateful for:

_____
_____
_____
_____

What I have learned from my challenges:

_____
_____
_____
_____

Three things (big or small) that went well today:

_____
_____
_____
_____

Three beautiful things that I have noticed throughout my day:

_____
_____
_____
_____

~You have infinite strength and power~

Date:_____

What I am grateful for:

_____
_____
_____
_____

What I have learned from my challenges:

_____
_____
_____
_____

Three things (big or small) that went well today:

_____
_____
_____
_____

Three beautiful things that I have noticed throughout my day:

_____
_____
_____
_____

~Choose kindness, choose love, choose peace~

Date:_____

What I am grateful for:

_____
_____
_____
_____

What I have learned from my challenges:

_____
_____
_____
_____

Three things (big or small) that went well today:

_____
_____
_____
_____

Three beautiful things that I have noticed throughout my day:

_____
_____
_____
_____

~Know who you are inside before anyone tries to tell you otherwise~

Date:_____

What I am grateful for:

_____
_____
_____
_____

What I have learned from my challenges:

_____
_____
_____
_____

Three things (big or small) that went well today:

_____
_____
_____
_____

Three beautiful things that I have noticed throughout my day:

_____
_____
_____
_____

~You are spectacular just for being you~

Date:_____

What I am grateful for:

_____
_____
_____
_____

What I have learned from my challenges:

_____
_____
_____
_____

Three things (big or small) that went well today:

_____
_____
_____
_____

Three beautiful things that I have noticed throughout my day:

_____
_____
_____
_____

~Appreciate every moment, even the bad, for the bad times force you to search within yourself in order to find true happiness~

Date:_____

What I am grateful for:

_____
_____
_____
_____

What I have learned from my challenges:

_____
_____
_____
_____

Three things (big or small) that went well today:

_____
_____
_____
_____

Three beautiful things that I have noticed throughout my day:

_____
_____
_____
_____

~You cannot possibly live a life of joy if you don't experience sorrow~

Date:_____

What I am grateful for:

_____
_____
_____
_____

What I have learned from my challenges:

_____
_____
_____
_____

Three things (big or small) that went well today:

_____
_____
_____
_____

Three beautiful things that I have noticed throughout my day:

_____
_____
_____
_____

~The issue that holds you back has nothing to do with who you are, it has to do with who you think you're not~

Date:_____

What I am grateful for:

_____
_____
_____
_____

What I have learned from my challenges:

_____
_____
_____
_____

Three things (big or small) that went well today:

_____
_____
_____
_____

Three beautiful things that I have noticed throughout my day:

_____
_____
_____
_____

~Stay positive, work hard and make it happen~

Date:_____

What I am grateful for:

_____
_____
_____
_____

What I have learned from my challenges:

_____
_____
_____
_____

Three things (big or small) that went well today:

_____
_____
_____
_____

Three beautiful things that I have noticed throughout my day:

_____
_____
_____
_____

~Be who you are, happiness comes from being your true authentic self~

Date:_____

What I am grateful for:

_____
_____
_____
_____

What I have learned from my challenges:

_____
_____
_____
_____

Three things (big or small) that went well today:

_____
_____
_____
_____

Three beautiful things that I have noticed throughout my day:

_____
_____
_____
_____

~When you dwell on what you don't have instead of what you do have,
you misunderstand life~

Date:_____

What I am grateful for:

_____
_____
_____
_____

What I have learned from my challenges:

_____
_____
_____
_____

Three things (big or small) that went well today:

_____
_____
_____
_____

Three beautiful things that I have noticed throughout my day:

_____
_____
_____
_____

~Be a leader, set a great example for others to follow~

Date:_____

What I am grateful for:

_____
_____
_____
_____

What I have learned from my challenges:

_____
_____
_____
_____

Three things (big or small) that went well today:

_____
_____
_____
_____

Three beautiful things that I have noticed throughout my day:

_____
_____
_____
_____

~Live a life of integrity, of purpose, of gratitude~

Date:_____

What I am grateful for:

_____
_____
_____
_____

What I have learned from my challenges:

_____
_____
_____
_____

Three things (big or small) that went well today:

_____
_____
_____
_____

Three beautiful things that I have noticed throughout my day:

_____
_____
_____
_____

~Choose to excel and not compete~

Date:_____

What I am grateful for:

_____
_____
_____
_____

What I have learned from my challenges:

_____
_____
_____
_____

Three things (big or small) that went well today:

_____
_____
_____
_____

Three beautiful things that I have noticed throughout my day:

_____
_____
_____
_____

~Happiness comes to those who are true to themselves, regardless of what others think~

Date:_____

What I am grateful for:

_____
_____
_____
_____

What I have learned from my challenges:

_____
_____
_____
_____

Three things (big or small) that went well today:

_____
_____
_____
_____

Three beautiful things that I have noticed throughout my day:

_____
_____
_____
_____

~Live a life of passion, do what makes you feel good~

Date:_____

What I am grateful for:

_____
_____
_____
_____

What I have learned from my challenges:

_____
_____
_____
_____

Three things (big or small) that went well today:

_____
_____
_____
_____

Three beautiful things that I have noticed throughout my day:

_____
_____
_____
_____

~Be thankful for your talents and use them to help other people~

Date:_____

What I am grateful for:

_____
_____
_____
_____

What I have learned from my challenges:

_____
_____
_____
_____

Three things (big or small) that went well today:

_____
_____
_____
_____

Three beautiful things that I have noticed throughout my day:

_____
_____
_____
_____

~Your life is like a blank book, no one else should write your story but you~

Date:_____

What I am grateful for:

_____
_____
_____
_____

What I have learned from my challenges:

_____
_____
_____
_____

Three things (big or small) that went well today:

_____
_____
_____
_____

Three beautiful things that I have noticed throughout my day:

_____
_____
_____
_____

~At times we focus so much on the things we don't want, that we forget to appreciate all that we do have~

Date:_____

What I am grateful for:

_____
_____
_____
_____

What I have learned from my challenges:

_____
_____
_____
_____

Three things (big or small) that went well today:

_____
_____
_____
_____

Three beautiful things that I have noticed throughout my day:

_____
_____
_____
_____

~Contentment is the result of living life with appreciation, love and gratitude~

Date:_____

What I am grateful for:

_____
_____
_____
_____

What I have learned from my challenges:

_____
_____
_____
_____

Three things (big or small) that went well today:

_____
_____
_____
_____

Three beautiful things that I have noticed throughout my day:

_____
_____
_____
_____

~People will come into your life as either blessings or lessons, either way, it benefits your personal growth~

Date:_____

What I am grateful for:

_____
_____
_____
_____

What I have learned from my challenges:

_____
_____
_____
_____

Three things (big or small) that went well today:

_____
_____
_____
_____

Three beautiful things that I have noticed throughout my day:

_____
_____
_____
_____

~Be thankful for the journey along with the end result~

Date:_____

What I am grateful for:

_____
_____
_____
_____

What I have learned from my challenges:

_____
_____
_____
_____

Three things (big or small) that went well today:

_____
_____
_____
_____

Three beautiful things that I have noticed throughout my day:

_____
_____
_____
_____

~Start treating yourself the way you want others to treat you~

Date:_____

What I am grateful for:

_____
_____
_____
_____

What I have learned from my challenges:

_____
_____
_____
_____

Three things (big or small) that went well today:

_____
_____
_____
_____

Three beautiful things that I have noticed throughout my day:

_____
_____
_____
_____

~Having courage doesn't mean you aren't afraid, courage is having fear and doing it regardless~

Date:_____

What I am grateful for:

_____
_____
_____
_____

What I have learned from my challenges:

_____
_____
_____
_____

Three things (big or small) that went well today:

_____
_____
_____
_____

Three beautiful things that I have noticed throughout my day:

_____
_____
_____
_____

~Whatever you believe is the truth~

Date:_____

What I am grateful for:

_____
_____
_____
_____

What I have learned from my challenges:

_____
_____
_____
_____

Three things (big or small) that went well today:

_____
_____
_____
_____

Three beautiful things that I have noticed throughout my day:

_____
_____
_____
_____

~Learn to enjoy the simple things in life~

My 30 Day Progression

My achievements in the last 30 days:

_____
_____
_____
_____
_____

How I perceive life differently today since the last 30 days:

_____
_____
_____
_____
_____

How I am more optimistic today since the last 30 days:

_____
_____
_____
_____
_____

What I have attracted into my life in the last 30 days:

_____
_____
_____
_____
_____

~We tend to look outside of ourselves for reassurance, happiness, love and support, when we truly understand that all of these things are already within us, we reach an incredible level of peace and freedom~

Nearly 6 months has gone by and you are definitely an entirely different person than you were 6 months ago.
You are an optimist who is grateful for everything you have. You now subconsciously search for the positive things in life and when obstacles fall in your path, they are never bigger than you.

In fact, you appreciate them now, because you know that every time you get through a challenge or face your fear, it only makes you stronger and more knowledgeable than you were before the discomfort.

Six months ago, you made a conscious decision to focus on the positive and since what you focus on grows, you have undoubtedly attracted many more things to be grateful for. Congratulations on this spiritual journey so far and I wish you many more blessings to come!

Love Julia

For a free PDF version of my Self Confidence Journal For Women, type the link below into your internet browser

http://eepurl.com/bXkMuv

Our website:
www.beautifulhealthymom.com

For more books:
http://www.beautifulhealthymom.com/our-products/

Julia Broderick Social Media:

Youtube:
https://www.youtube.com/user/beautifulhealthymom1

Facebook:
https://www.facebook.com/BeautifulHealthyMom/

Twitter:
https://twitter.com/Beautyhealthmom

Printed in Great Britain
by Amazon